KEY

- Wildf[...] [...] and organized
  withi[...]
- Leaf att[...] [...] next to each wildflower.
- Descriptions include important facts such as cluster shape, number of petals, or center color to help you quickly identify the species. Size information is sometimes included as well.

LEAF ATTACHMENT

Wildflower leaves attach to stems in different ways. The leaf icons next to the flowers show alternate, opposite, whorled, perfoliate, clasping, and basal attachments. Some wildflower plants have two or more types of leaf attachments.

 ALTERNATE leaves attach in an alternating pattern.

 OPPOSITE leaves attach directly opposite each other.

 BASAL leaves originate at the base of the plant and are usually grouped in pairs or in a rosette.

 PERFOLIATE leaves are stalkless and have a leaf base that completely surrounds the main stem.

 CLASPING leaves have no stalk, and the base partly surrounds the main stem.

 WHORLED leaves have three or more leaves that attach around the stem at the same point.

 CLUSTERED leaves originate from the same point on the stem.

 SPINES are leaves that take the form of sharp spines.

PARTS OF A FLOWER

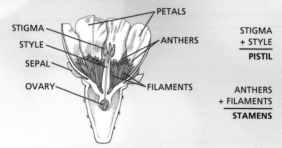

STIGMA
STYLE
SEPAL
OVARY

PETALS
ANTHERS
FILAMENTS

STIGMA
+ STYLE
PISTIL

ANTHERS
+ FILAMENTS
STAMENS

CLIMATE, GEOGRAPHY, AND PLANT DIVERSITY

Bisected by a conglomerate of mountain ranges uplifted by shifting tectonic plates, southern California sits squeezed between cold Pacific currents and blazing deserts. The Coastal Ranges run parallel to the coastline and impede the cool, Pacific moisture from flowing eastward. Conversely, the Transverse Ranges angle east-west and channel ocean moisture inland. The continent's hottest, driest deserts exist on the east side of the Peninsula Ranges and Sierra Nevadas, and the rare, sub-tropical Mediterranean climate bathes the seaward side. The Mediterranean Climate, with its cool, rainy winters contrasted with either a hot-dry summer (south coast) or cool-dry summer (central coast), exists in only five regions in the world besides the Mediterranean. The wide divergence of climate, geology, and geography creates a region with one of the greatest biodiversities in North America.

With elevations ranging from 227 feet below sea level (Salton Sea) in the Colorado Desert to 11,485 feet high in the San Bernardino Mountains (Mount San Gorgonio), southern California encompasses an extraordinary variety of plant communities. Each major vegetative province supports a unique community of plants adapted to its specific environmental conditions. Within a few miles, growing conditions vary from the breezy south coast that never freezes (Long Beach to San Diego), through transitional grasslands rich with wildflowers, to blazing deserts that receive less than 5 inches of rain annually and sunbaked mountain slopes with cacti and yucca, which are followed in turn by snowy mountain meadows. With species derived from deserts, tropics, and alpine tundra, southern California includes more than 2,200 species of vascular plants as well as about 700 naturalized introduced species.

Amsinckia intermedia

Common Fiddleneck

Stem 1–3 feet tall, hairy; flower spike curved with tiny tubular flowers; leaves narrow, hairy

Ericameria nauseosa

Rubber Rabbitbrush

Shrub 3–6 feet tall; dense clusters of tiny disk flowers, no rays; leaves narrow or absent

Eriogonum umbellatum

Sulfur Flower Buckwheat

Flowers on 8–12-inch stems; leaf-like bracts at branching nodes; leaves oval, woolly underneath

Eriogonum inflatum

Desert Trumpet

Distinctive inflated stems to 20 inches tall; small flower clusters on erect shoots; leaves rounded

Eriophyllum confertiflorum

Golden Yarrow

Stout, woolly white stems 8–24 inches tall; dense flower clusters; leaves narrow, deeply lobed

Hymenopappus filifolius

Columbia Cutleaf

Stems to 40 inches; flowerheads a cluster of tiny tubular florets; leaves have threadlike lobes

Solidago velutina

Three-nerve Goldenrod

Stems 6–30 inches tall with slender clusters of tiny flowers; leaves taper to base and tip

Tribulus terrestris

Puncture Vine

Stems sprawling; leaves with small leaflets along midrib; nutlets have stout, sharp spines

Descurainia sophia

Flixweed

Leafy stem to 25 inches; cluster of tiny flowers; seedpods linear, erect around stem; leaf fern-like

Orobanche fasciculata

no leaves

Clustered Broomrape

Clusters of 6-inch flower stalks each have one yellowish to pinkish-purple, tubular flower

Bahiopsis parishii

Parish Goldeneye

Shrubby; flowerheads with 5–18 pointed rays around disk; leaves rough and hairy, edges toothed

Baileya multiradiata

Desert Marigold

Showy flowers have 30–60 notched rays around a disk; leaves deeply lobed, fuzzy-woolly

Coreopsis californica

California Coreopsis

Stems to 8 inches tall, mostly leafless; flowerhead with 8 notched rays; leaves with narrow lobes

Ehrendorferia chrysantha

Golden Eardrops

Stems to 5 feet tall; 2 curving outer petals, 2 erect central petals; leaves with fern-like lobes

Erysimum capitatum

Wallflower

Rounded clusters of reddish orange or yellow flowers; tall stems; long seedpods erect around stem

Gutierrezia sarothrae

Broom Snakeweed

Round with dense branches; 1–2 feet tall; small flowers with 3–8 rays; yellow disk; threadlike leaves

Hypericum scouleri

St. John's Wort

Stems 7–27 inches tall; 5 petals lined with black dots and numerous stamens; found in moist soils

Mentzelia albicaulis

Whitestem Blazing Star

Stems 12 inches tall; flowers on hairy cylinder that becomes a fruit capsule; leaves with barbed hairs

Mimulus guttatus

Yellow Monkeyflower

Tubular flowers, heavily bearded middle lobe has red spots; leaves oval; found in wet habitats

Potentilla anserina

Silverweed Cinquefoil

Prostrate with red runners; flowers with 5 petals on leafless stalk; leaves with leaflets along midrib

Pectis papposa

Common Chinchweed

Mounding clumps; small flowerheads; 8 rays around yellow disk; narrow leaves; lemon-scented

Peritoma arborea

Bladderpod

Shrubby, ill-smelling; flowers with 4 petals, fruit an inflated pod; leaves with 3 narrow leaflets

Ranunculus californicus

California Buttercup

Stems 1–2 feet tall; flowers with 9–17 petals, many stamens; leaves with 3 oval, hairy, pointed lobes

Ribes aureum

Golden Currant

Thornless shrub 6–9 feet tall; clusters of flowers with 5 pointed petals; berries orange, no prickles

Senecio flaccidus

Threadleaf Ragwort

Leafy stems 1–4 feet tall; clusters of 3–10 flowerheads with 8–13 rays each; leaves threadlike

Sphaeralcea ambigua

Apricot Globemallow

Stems 20–40 inches tall; cuplike flowers red-orange to pink, lavender, white; triangular, lobed leaves

Stanleya pinnata

Prince's Plume

Stems 1–4 feet tall; spikes of tubular flowers, petals slender, stamens extended; lance-shaped leaves

Verbascum thapsus

Mullein

Stems to 6 feet; spikes of yellow flowers, 5 petals; leaves large, fuzzy; roadside invasive

Viola pedunculata

California Golden Violet

Clusters of stems up to 15 inches tall; lower 3 petals with brown lines; leaves oval to variable

Encelia californica

Coast Sunflower

Bushy; flowers on long, hairy stems; rays notched; disk brown or yellow; leaves green

Encelia farinosa

Brittlebush

Bushy; flowers on long, yellowish, hairless stems; disk brown or yellow; leaves woolly, silvery

Heterotheca villosa

Hairy Golden Aster

Hairy stems to 20 inches tall; flowerheads with 7–21 rays; leaves short, hairy, widely spaced

Grindelia hirsutula

Hairy Gumweed

Hairy stems to 12 inches tall; flower with yellow rays and disk on base lined with tiny hooks

Lasthenia californica

California Goldfields

Stems to 16 inches tall; flower-heads with 6–13 notched rays; disk yellow; can carpet landscapes

Malacothrix glabrata

Desert Dandelion

Hairless stems to 15 inches tall with few leaves; flowerheads with 30–100 toothed rays; milky sap

Nicotiana glauca

Tree Tobacco

Tree 6–20 feet; flowers yellow-green, tubular, narrow; leaves blue-green, oval; all parts toxic

Verbesina encelioides

Golden Crownbeard

Branching stems to 20 inches tall; flowerheads with 12–15 notched rays; yellow disk; toothed leaves

Papaver californicum

Fire Poppy

Stems to 2 feet, blooms after fires; 4 orange petals with greenish basal spot, showy stamens; sap milky

Abutilon palmeri

Palmer's Indian Mallow

Shrubby plants with velvety, heart-shaped leaves; flowers orange with 5 rounded petals

Agave shawii

Coastal Agave

Flowers in flat, dense clusters on 12 foot tall stalks; leaves sword-like with cat-claw spines

Dendromecon rigida

Bush Poppy

Shrubby to 9 feet tall; flowers with 4 fan-shaped petals; showy stamens; lance-shaped leaves

Layia platyglossa

Coastal Tidytips

Stems to 2 feet tall; flowers with 5–18 rays that are two-tone (rarely solid) with 3 notches; yellow disk

Oenothera elata

Evening Primrose

Leafy, branching stems to 8 feet; funnel-shaped flowers; 4 showy petals; upper leaves get smaller

Tragopogon dubius

Yellow Salsify, Goatsbeard

Flowers with green phyllaries longer than rays; seedhead is a feathery sphere; grass-like leaves

Fremontodendron californicum

Flannelbush

Shrub; flowers to 3 inches wide with showy stamens; leaves have broad lobes, hairy

Helianthus annuus

Common Sunflower

Stems to 9 feet, branching; flower rays yellow, disk brown to yellow; leaves heart-shaped

Calochortus clavatus

Clubhair Mariposa Lily

Zigzag stems with grass-like leaves; flowers with 3 petals and a reddish band with long hairs

Leptosyne gigantea

Giant Coreopsis

Shrubby to 6 feet tall; flowerheads with 10–16 rays and a yellow disk; leaves filament-like

Cucurbita foetidissima

Stinking Gourd

Sprawling stems; flowers with
5 large petals; fruit a green-striped
ball; leaves scratchy, ill-smelling

Eschscholzia californica

California Poppy

Flowers blanket hillsides with
4 gold-to-orange petals; leaves
with fern-like lobes; yellow sap

Mentzelia laevicaulis

Giant Blazing Star

Stems to 40 inches; flowers 3–6
inches wide, many showy stamens;
leaves lobed, sandpapery

Ferocactus cylindraceus

California Barrel Cactus

Barrel stem; ribbed, up to 6 feet
tall; yellow flowers circle top;
spines slightly curved, multicolored

Opuntia engelmannii

Engelmann's Prickly Pear

Shrubby; up to 9 feet tall; pads
with rows of white spines; flowers
solid yellow; juicy red fruit

Opuntia littoralis

Coastal Prickly Pear

Shrubby to 3 feet high; flowers
yellow with red style in center
topped with green lobes; fruit red

Opuntia phaeacantha

Brown-spine Prickly Pear

Clumps of bluish-green pads, upper half with white to dark-brown
spines; petals yellow with red base

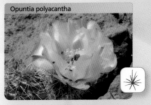
Opuntia polyacantha

Plains Prickly Pear

Spreads along ground with con-
nected, spiny pads; petals solid
yellow; fruit a dry, tan capsule

Abronia villosa

Hairy Sand-Verbena

Round clusters of tubular, pink to reddish flowers; prostrate to erect, hairy stems

Persicaria amphibia

Water Smartweed

Plants of shallow water and marshy soils; tiny flowers in dense, cylindrical spikes above water

Allionia incarnata

Trailing Four-O'Clock/ Pink Windmills

Low, sprawling stems spread 1–3 feet; small, rose to pink flowers

Clarkia purpurea

Winecup Clarkia

Stems 1–3 feet tall; flowers bowl-shaped with 4 lavender-to-pink or deep red, fan-shaped petals

Dudleya pulverulenta

Chalk Dudleya

A dense rosette of succulent, ash-colored, pointed leaves; red flowers waxy with fused petals

Epilobium canum

California Fuchsia

Shrubby; red to orange, tubular flowers with lobed, spreading petals, protruding stamens

Eremalche rotundifolia

Desert Fivespot

Stems to 2 feet tall; bowl-shaped flowers pink to lavender; 5 petals with a dark red spot near the base

Fouquieria splendens

Ocotillo

Stems 8–20 feet tall, thorny, and whip-like; flowers tubular, clustered on stem tips; leaves usually absent

Linanthus californicus

Prickly Phlox

Prickly stems to 3 feet tall; funnel-shaped flowers have 5 petals, a white base and a yellow throat

Linanthus dianthiflorus

Ground Pink

Funnel-shaped flowers with 5 pink to white toothed lobes, a white to maroon base, and a yellow throat

Malacothamnus fasciculatus

Chaparral Bush Mallow

Shrub to 15 feet, stems white-hairy; 5 petals, pale-pink; leaves oval to lobed, soft-hairy, veined

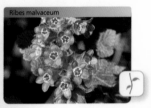
Ribes malvaceum

Chaparral Currant

Thornless shrub 3–6 feet tall; pink to whitish dangling tubular flowers; berries purplish, no prickles

Ribes speciosum

Fuchsia-flowered Gooseberry

Dangling scarlet tubular flowers, reddish berries densely prickly

Silene laciniata

Cardinal Catchfly

Stems branching; 1–2 feet tall; tubular flowers with 5 deeply cut petals with pointed lobes

Aquilegia formosa

Western Columbine

Stems to 2 feet tall; nodding red flowers have yellow-tipped petals and long, straight, red spurs

Castilleja miniata

Scarlet Paintbrush

Spikes of red bracts lobed like pitchforks surround small, yellowish, beak-shaped flowers

Castilleja chromosa

Desert Paintbrush

Lobed, hairy, red-tipped bracts and small, yellow, beak-like flowers; pointed lobes on upper leaves

Epipactis gigantea

Giant Helleborine Orchid

Leafy stems to 3 feet tall bear up to 18 flowers; the lower petal wiggles in the breeze

Justicia californica

Chuparosa

Shrubby to 6 feet tall; tubular red flower with drooping lip; often leafless when blooming

Pedicularis densiflora

Indian Warrior

Stems to 20 inches tall; a dense spike of showy tubular flowers and bracts; leaves fern-like

Penstemon eatonii

Firecracker Penstemon

2-foot stems; scarlet flowers in a one-sided spike are tubular with small, rounded, equal-sized lobes

Rosa californica

California Rose

Thicket-forming shrub with prickles; flowers have 5 pink-reddish petals and showy yellow stamens

Salvia spathacea

Hummingbird Sage

Mat-forming; bloom spikes have whorls of tubular flowers with drooping lower lips

Calochortus kennedyi

Desert Mariposa Lily

Red-orange to yellow flowers; 3 rounded petals with hairy, dark basal band; grass-like leaves

Diplacus aurantiacus

Coryphantha vivipara

Sticky Monkeyflower

Shrubby; paired tubular flowers, 5 petals, yellow to orange or red; narrow leaves hairy, sticky beneath

Spinystar Cactus

Cylindrical stems covered with spiny tubercles; flowers grow on stem tip; fruit oval, greenish

Cylindropuntia acanthocarpa

Opuntia basilaris

Buckhorn Cholla

Spiny, cylindrical branches; flowers bronze to yellow or red; red filaments and yellow anthers

Beavertail Cactus

Blue-green pads without long spines; flowers with red filaments, yellow anthers, white stigmas

Echinocereus engelmannii

Echinocereus triglochidiatus

Engelmann Hedgehog Cactus

Cylindric stems to 18 inches tall, 4 inches wide; petal tips pointed

Mojave Kingcup Cactus

Red-to-orange petals with rounded tips; cylindrical stems to 18 inches tall; 3-11 spines per areole

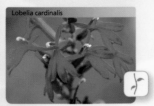
Lobelia cardinalis

Delphinium cardinale

Cardinal Flower

Moisture-loving plant; stems 2–6 feet tall; flowers tubular, lobes spreading, pointed

Scarlet Larkspur

Stems to 6 feet; widely spaced flowers; spreading, long spur; radiating lobes on leaves

White to Green

Abronia turbinata

White Sand-Verbena
Erect to sprawling stems; dense spheres of small, tubular flowers; leaves oval to heart-shaped; hairy

Achillea millefolium

Common Yarrow
Flat to rounded clusters of tiny, white flowers crown 1–3-foot stems; leaves aromatic, fernlike

Anemopsis californica

Yerba Mansa
Wetland plant; spike with 4–9 white, petal-like bracts below cone with smaller white bracts

Apocynum androsaemifolium

Spreading Dogbane
Erect 8–40-inch-tall branching stems; bell-shaped flowers in slightly nodding clusters

Arctostaphylos glauca

Big-berry Manzanita
Shrub to 24 feet tall; red bark; clusters of urn-shaped flowers, fruit red to black; leaves oblong

Asclepias fascicularis

Narrow-leaf Milkweed
Stems to 3 feet tall; round clusters of small, creamy-pink flowers; leaves narrow; milky sap

Brickellia californica

California Brickellbush
Large, leafy shrubs; tubular flowers tassel-like, creamy-greenish; triangular to oval leaves

Cneoridium dumosum

Bush Rue
Aromatic shrub to 5 feet; fruit a reddish berry; leaves linear, gold in summer; common near San Diego

Conium maculatum

Poison Hemlock

Tall, red-streaked stems, rounded flower clusters; leaves resemble parsley; **deadly poisonous**

Daucus pusillus

American Wild Carrot

Stem 12–36 inches tall; umbrella-like flower cluster of smaller round clusters; leaves resemble parsley

Corallorhiza maculata

no leaves

Spotted Coralroot Orchid

Stems leafless, red or yellow, and pencil-thin; red spots on flower lower lip; occurs in forests

Cryptantha clevelandii

Common Cryptantha

Densely hairy stems; curling cluster of tiny flowers with 5 rounded petal lobes and a yellow throat

Draba cuneifolia

Wedge-leaf Draba

Stem hairy, 2–12 inches tall; small flowers with 4 petals; pods flat, oblong; leaves hairy

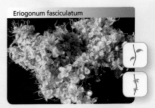
Eriogonum fasciculatum

California Buckwheat

Shrub to 6 feet tall; white to pink flowers, petals with/without a pink midstripe; linear leaves in clusters

Eriogonum wrightii

Wright's Buckwheat

Shrubby; flowers in linear clusters, petals white-pinkish with red mid-stripe; leaves elliptic, woolly

Eriogonum nudum

Naked Buckwheat

Stems leafless, to 16-inches; round clusters of white to pink flowers; leaves elliptic, woolly below

White to Green

Lepidium virginicum

Peppergrass
Clustered stems to 2 feet tall; dense clusters of small flowers with 4 petals; seeds circle stem

Maianthemum stellatum

Star Solomon's Seal
Each short branch of clusters has a star-shaped flower with 6 narrow petals; leaves sword-like

Lathyrus vestitus

Pacific Peavine
Twinning vine; flower's upper banner petal has red lines; leaflets on midrib tipped with tendrils

Prunus virginiana

Chokecherry
Shrubby tree; flowers in cylindric clusters; fruit reddish-black; serrated lance-shaped leaves

Sambucus nigra

Blue Elderberry
Shrub/small tree; flat-topped flower clusters; fruit blue-black; leaves with 3–9 leaflets along midrib

Solanum physalifolium

Hoe Nightshade
Stems to 30 inches tall; flowers small with 5 star-like petals, yellow anthers; berries yellow-greenish

Clematis ligusticifolia

Western Virgin's Bower
Vine; flowers with 5 hairy petals, showy stamens; leaves have 5 leaflets; fruit a silky plume

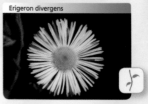
Erigeron divergens

Spreading Fleabane
White to lavender-tinted rays around a yellow disk; branching stems; buds nod; narrow leaves

White to Green

Erigeron philadelphicus

Philadelphia Fleabane

Leafy, hairy stems to 30 inches tall; flowerheads with 150-plus white rays; clasping upper leaves

Fragaria vesca

Wild Strawberry

Small, white flowers and red fruits; basal leaves with 3 leaflets with coarse teeth

Glycyrrhiza lepidota

Wild Licorice

Stems leafy, 1–4 feet tall; seed-pods covered with hooked prickles; leaves have 13–19 leaflets

Marah macrocarpa

Wild Cucumber

Vine; flowers with 5 hairy petals; fruit egg-shaped with prickles; leaves hairy, deeply cut lobes

Nicotiana obtusifolia

Desert Tobacco

Sticky-hairy, to 3 feet tall; flowers funnel-shaped, creamy to green-white; oval to lance-shaped leaves

Oenothera suffrutescens

Wild Honeysuckle

Stems hairy to 20 inches tall; spikes of flowers with 4 spoon-like white petals, fading to red

Platanthera dilatata

Tall White Bog Orchid

Stems to 45 inches tall in wet areas; petals spread out with an upper hood, a drooping lower lip

Veratrum californicum

Corn Lily

Small flowers on branching stalks; tall, cornlike stems in moist areas; broad, strongly veined leaves

White to Green

Calycoseris wrightii

White Tackstem

Stems 8 inches tall; rays toothed, red stripes on backside; deeply lobed leaves; milky sap

Convolvulus arvensis

Field Bindweed

Prostate stems to 6 feet long; pink to white funnel-shaped flowers; oval to lance-shaped leaves

Cylindropuntia bigelovii

Teddy Bear Cholla

Shrubby; covered with straw-colored spines; flowers pale green, filaments green, anthers orange

Heliotropium convolvulaceum

Phlox Heliotrope

Sand-loving, 4–16 inches tall, sprawling stems; petals united, 5-sided with tiny yellow throat

Toxicoscordion fremontii

Fremont's Death Camas

Stem to 2 feet tall; flowers star-like; 6 petals with green basal dots; leaves slender, arching

Calystegia macrostegia

Island Morning Glory

Twinning vine with funnel-shaped, white to pinkish flowers; triangular leaves

Argemone munita

Prickly Poppy

Tall stem and leaves prickly; flowers with large, delicate petals and showy yellow stamens

Oenothera caespitosa

Tufted Evening Primrose

Sprawling stems; flowers with 4 heart-shaped petals and slender, pointed, hairy buds

White to Green

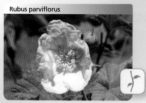
Rubus parviflorus

Thimbleberry

Low, leafy, thornless shrub; flowers have 5 petals, showy yellow stamens; berries red, edible

Hesperoyucca whipplei

Chaparral Yucca

Trunkless, yucca-like; flowers on 8 foot stalk; basal leaves 1–3-feet long, spear-like

Yucca baccata

Banana Yucca

Trunkless; long dagger-like leaves lined with shredding threads; flower cluster mostly within leaves

Yucca schidigera

Mojave Yucca

Trunks to 15 feet tall tipped with dense clusters of flowers; leaves dagger-like, lined with threads

Yucca brevifolia

Joshua Tree Yucca

Branching trunk to 45 feet tall tipped with dense flower clusters; dagger-like leaves lack threads

Datura wrightii

Sacred Datura

Robust, sprawling plant, 5 feet across; flowers trumpet-shaped; leaves oval to 10 inches long

Hesperocallis undulata

Desert Lily

Stems 12–20 inches tall; flowers with 6 white to yellowish petals; leaves folded, edges wavy, white

Romneya coulteri

Coulter's Matilija Poppy

California's largest flower; stems to 7 feet tall, flower 8 inches wide; leaves lobed along midrib

Cirsium vulgare

Bull Thistle
Stems to 6 feet tall; spiny heads with clusters of purple, tassel-like flowers; leaves spiny

Mirabilis albida

Velvet Umbrellawort
Stems hairy to 40 inches tall; pale-pink to violet flowers have extended stamens

Mirabilis multiflora

Giant Four O'clock
Sprawling densely branching stems; clusters of 6 magenta flowers, one opens each afternoon

Amorpha fruticosa

False Indigo
Shrub; erect spikes of small, purple flowers with yellow anthers; 9–25 oval leaflets along midrib

Astragalus lentiginosus

Freckled Milkvetch
Clumps to 3 feet wide; reddish, sprawling stems and spikes of purple and white, tubular flowers

Collinsia heterophylla

Purple Chinese Houses
Stems to 2 feet tall; snapdragon-like flowers with purple lower and pale to white upper petals

Delphinium parishii

Desert Larkspur
Pale to dark-blue, white, or pink flowers with tufts of hair and tiny spurs; leaves with radiating lobes

Dichelostemma capitatum

Blue Dicks/Wild Hyacinth
Rounded clusters of tubular flowers with 6 petals ranging from bluish-purple to pink; grass-like leaves

Dieteria canescens

Purple Aster

Flower clusters on 2-foot stems; heads crowded with slender, blue to purple rays, disk yellow

Erodium texanum

Desert Heron's Bill

Reddish stems erect to sprawling; 5 showy magenta petals, seed-pods taper like a bird's bill

Gilia capitata

Bluehead Gilia

Dense, rounded clusters of flowers have 5 petals and extended stamens; fern-like leaves

Linum lewisii

Blue Flax

Flowers with 5 delicate petals last only one day; narrow, pointed leaves hug the stem

Lupinus sparsiflorus

Mojave Lupine

Stems hairy; 6–8 inch long spikes of tubular flowers; leaves have 7–11 radiating, hairy lobes

Lupinus succulentus

Arroyo Lupine

Leafy stems; 3–6 inch spikes of tubular flowers; leaves have 7–9 radiating, hairless lobes

Lamium amplexicaule

Henbit

Square stems 2–14 inches tall; flower purple to pink, tubular; leaves rounded; common lawn weed

Pholistoma auritum

Fiesta Flower

Stems square, prickly and clinging; flowers with 5 lobes and dark throat spots; clasping leaves

Salvia clevelandii

Cleveland Sage

Square stems to 5 feet tall; whorled clusters of tubular flowers with spreading lips

Sisyrinchium bellum

Western Blue-eyed Grass

Dense clumps of flat, grass-like leaves; flower has a yellow throat, 6 petals with pointed tips

Solanum elaeagnifolium

Silverleaf Nightshade

Stems and leaves prickly, covered with matted silvery hairs; flowers star-shaped; fruit a yellow berry

Solanum xanti

Chaparral Nightshade

Shrubby, 3 feet tall; petals blue; disk with a green base; fruit a greenish berry; leaves dark green

Vicia americana

American Vetch

Low-climbing vine; spikes have 1–9 narrow, tubular flowers; leaves with leaflets along midrib

Viola adunca

Hooked-spur Violet

Flowers blue to violet; whitish throats have dark lines; basal leaves oval to triangular

Zeltnera venusta

Charming Centaury

Branching stem to 20 inches tall; flowers have 5 pointed petals, white throat; oval to narrow leaves

Castilleja exserta

Purple Owl's Clover

Stems hairy; spikes of lobed, rose-purple bracts surround yellow- to white-tipped flowers

Eriastrum densifolium

Giant Woollystar
Stems 4–16 inches tall; clusters of 10–20 blue to lavender, funnel-shaped flowers

Nemophila menziesii

Baby Blue Eyes
Stem to 12 inches tall; flower a bowl with 5 rounded, shallow lobes and a white center

Phacelia campanularia

Desert Bluebells
Stems to 2 feet tall; flowers bell-shaped with a white throat, blue filaments, and white anthers

Symphyotrichum ascendens

Western Aster
Hairy stems to 2 feet tall; flower-heads with 15–40 narrow, purplish rays; disk yellow; leaves narrow

Trichostema lanatum

Woolly Blue Curls
Shrubby; flowers hairy with 5 spreading lobes, 4 arching purple stamens; leaves narrow, clustered

Eustoma exaltatum

Catchfly Prairie Gentian
Stems 20–30 inches tall; 5 purple to lavender petals with dark bases and yellow-tipped anthers

Iris missouriensis

Missouri Iris
Classic iris flower with blue and white, blue-streaked petals; leaves flat, long, slender

Cirsium occidentale

Western (Woolly) Thistle
Stems woolly, 6–8 feet tall; tassel-like flowers lavender, purple, red, or white on woolly, prickly base

Only Southern California Wildflowers

Organized by color for quick and easy identification

Simple and convenient—narrow your choices by color and leaf attachment, and view just a few wildflowers at a time

- Pocket-size format—easier than laminated foldouts
- Professional photos of flowers in bloom
- Similar colors grouped together to ensure that you quickly find what you're looking for
- Leaf icons for comparison and identification
- Easy-to-use information for even casual observers
- Expert author is a skilled botanist and photographer

Get these *Adventure Quick Guides* for your area

$9.95

Adventure Publications
820 Cleveland Street South
Cambridge, Minnesota 55008
(800) 678-7006
www.adventurepublications.net
NATURE/WILDFLOWERS/CALIFORNIA

ISBN 978-1-59193-751-7

5 0 9 9 5

9 781591 937517